The Tree Poets

River of Stone

Peter Burrows

Phil Vernon

Tista Austin

First published 2025 by The Hedgehog Poetry Press

Published in the UK by
The Hedgehog Poetry Press
5, Coppack House
Churchill Avenue
Clevedon
BS21 6QW

www.hedgehogpress.co.uk

ISBN: 978-1-913499-88-4

Copyright © Mark Davidson 2025

The right of Mark Davidson to be identified as the editor of this work has been asserted in accordance with the Copyright, Designs and Patents Act 1988. All rights for individual works retained by the respective author.

All rights reserved. No part of this publication may be reproduced, stored in or introduced into a retrieval system, or transmitted in any form, or by any means (electronic, mechanical, photocopying, recording or otherwise) without prior written permissions of the publisher. Any person who does any unauthorised act in relation to this publication may be liable for criminal prosecution and civil claims for damages,

9 8 7 6 5 4 3 2 1

A CIP Catalogue record for this book is available from the British Library.

The Tree Poets

Peter Burrows 7

    The Old Routes 8
    The Hare on the Hill 9
    The Fallen Tree 10
    Across the Bay 11
    Quarry 12
    The Stone Kiss 13

Phil Vernon 15

    Unrest 17
    Earth 18
    Water 19
    Fire 20
    Air 21

Tista Austin 23

    Fen Orchid 25
    Schwanengesang 26
    Blue fen 27
    Another river path 28
    Feral 29

PETER BURROWS

THE OLD ROUTES

I'm developing your eye for spotting
from afar those grown over embankments
that run into nowhere. Those landscaped cuttings
strolled by horses and bikes on family Sundays,
near restored station houses, now quaint dwellings
or cafes. Their proud repainted signs conjuring up
the lost branch lines of your youth. Once explored

by that keen railway clerk, staff pass in hand;
determined to free-ride every outstretched
stretch of line. Steam, diesel, electric charged you
along the routes that became your life's frame.
Your work, and day trips transporting our lives
across the network, until we branched off onto
our own distant lines – still connected, yet,

retired, alone – pass in hand, time now your own,
you travel further back to past routes. The preserve
of a comforting ride; a relatable world,
absorbing your presence. Request stops expressed by
to interests beyond us. The postbag dangles
uncollected; swinging in the slipstream.
I could jump on a handcar, pushing up

and down the track, waving a red flag to catch you,
but, no, I fall back. Rolling to a halt.
As you continue unaware, always
some place to go on the railways of your mind.
Timetables you knew by heart still running,
almost on time. In the distance, small,
vivid as a commemorative stamp:

the grey-white plume billows out as ghost trains
fly across absent bridges. Glide through
bricked up tunnels over forgotten crossings.
Fingers turn over tickets to beyond
destinations stated. Trains, arrivals,
departures. Momentum still travelling.
You lean out the window. The wind in your hair.

THE HARE ON THE HILL

The grass is that bit longer.
It hides the hare on the hill
that I see when I pass at this time of day.
But I know that it's watching me, still.

THE FALLEN TREE

The winds had returned by the time
I finally got around to finding the spot
they had all been talking about.
On another day, it could have been one of any
silenced contender littering the muddy ridge.
But when I saw it, I knew. Fallen back
from the top bank onto the sloping field -
appearing as if mid-fall – its weight
taken by the land. Bushels flailing, grasping air,
writhing in the wind. I half-circled,
sizing its shapeless mass spread out
like a grounded hot-air balloon.

The nosing dog backed off
as it fanned alive once more.
Then ceased to stillness. Its fluttered feathers fell,
darkened. Had those across the water heard
its leafy collapse, its unseasonal crash?

Bending down to stroke the once sunned,
slipped crown that stood high
and anonymous among the lined crowd,

had I realised before what lives lived
in such an abundance of leaves -
almost stepping on the still-attached acorns
resting at my feet.

ACROSS THE BAY

Hest Bank, Morecambe

We take the day, just you and me,
driving about the family haunts
heading back towards the coast to where
you once holidayed, long before,

applying gloss to outworn memories.
Retouching this place and the past.
But why return? What have we left
behind? Across the bay the mist

layers outlines of the mountains.
Always seeming further away,
out of reach. But I know there must
be someone who still knows the safest route

across these ever-shifting sands.
Up high from the railway footbridge,
you film speeding trains to splice shots
before and after, fifty years

reconnected. Up beside you
I'm absorbed by the vast knowing sky
over the bay: the space that holds
nothing and everything. Light

altering the land and us; sun rays
breaking through - quick, bright patches like
once known, reawakened parts of the brain
scanned, illuminating on and off.

QUARRY

Over stretched wire, obscured in nettle,
a faltering warning sign leans to. Stumble
up rooted steps, onto a green clouded plain where
vague trenches run down a grassy crater
moating sheer rockface. Its scarred aspect recalls

a forgotten siege: explosions, collapsing
curtain walls, dust plumes, injured cries. Cutting
deeper into land. Spoils rising. Behind lines,
all weathers, the clatter and scrape, dressing stone.
Each hand uniquely marks their own piece work.

A bird song away, sandstone terraces rise as one.
The renowned flags lined to legacies beyond
Boulder Street, Rock Terrace, The Mason's Arms...
London, Europe. Eighty years working this outcrop;
permanent dust on windows. Blackened edges.

Which night was it, unannounced, 0400 hours,
Rawlinson's men, white paper in hand,
led the horses to the station, to the boats?
By dawn, fifty men let go. All ground to a halt.
How many followed knowing it was the end?

Such silent industry. Time relays, reclaims. Absence
grown over. A natural forgetting. Unmarked, mossed,
the last dropped blocks tumbled like dice, paused
an age. Millstone Grit to Anthropocene.
Across the field only the deer return.

THE STONE KISS

After 'Bucht, Mainland', Orkney, photographed by Gunnie Moberg (1979).

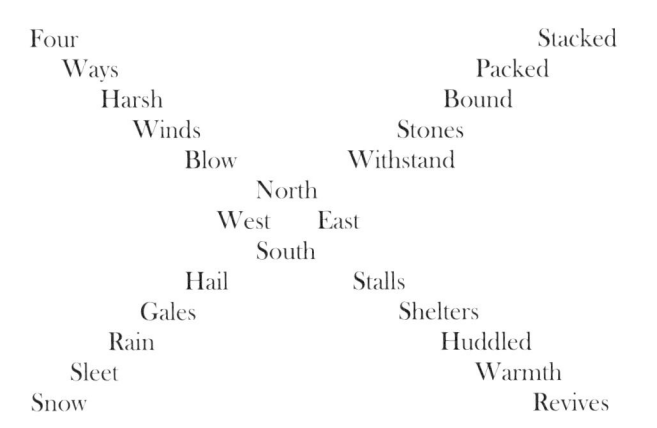

```
Four                              Stacked
  Ways                          Packed
    Harsh                     Bound
      Winds               Stones
        Blow          Withstand
            North
              West    East
            South
        Hail          Stalls
     Gales              Shelters
   Rain                   Huddled
 Sleet                      Warmth
Snow                          Revives
```

Brittle Star issue 6, July 2020

The Stone Kiss is inspired by Gunnie Moberg's aerial photograph of a drystone sheep shelter in Orkney, hence its form. Built like a cross: no matter which direction the wind, rain or snow was blowing, sheep could go into one corner of the cross and find shelter.

PHIL VERNON

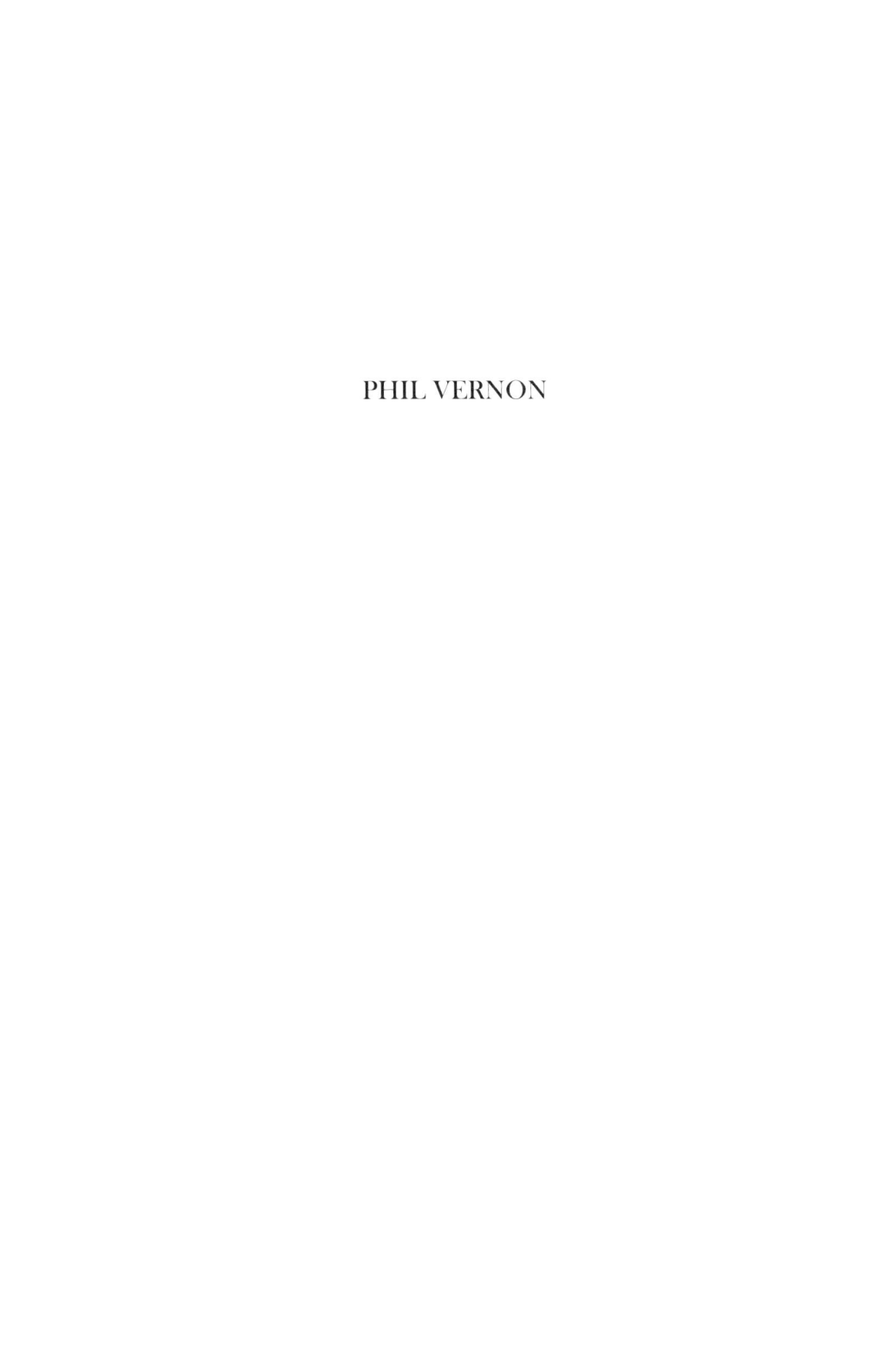

UNREST

We barely knew it was there,
hidden, feet beneath our feet,
as we walked to school and back,
along the market street.

And then, one day, it roused
and swelled and surged, until
it ripped and burst its bounds –
as captive water will –

and buckled pavements, tore
through tarmac, heaved concrete,
and floated market stalls
in water three feet deep.

They pass among our dead,
mix our detritus with their loam,
and, when their moment comes,
oust families from their homes;

and still, few know their names,
nor where these rivers flow –
buried by the city's needs,
unseen, unheard, below.

In 1968, the River Quaggy burst free of the tunnel to which it had been confined since Victorian times, flooding parts of SE London, and causing widespread damage.

EARTH

Shaping a world it doesn't know,
the planet spins at breakneck speed,
but all that matters, happens slow:
the giant rafts infringe the sea,

and drift, neither towards nor from,
but with a kind of purpose, yet –
as settled nomads have, who long
to roam again across the steppe –

till there's a chance they may collide,
and sensing thus to end the peace,
like magnets draw each other in,

to crumple, grind and merge, and rise
and make, from long held-in release,
these mountains, free of grace or sin.

WATER

These mountains, free of grace or sin,
are scourged by gravity, and rain
that never ends – their flesh and skin
eroded, softened, scoured, flayed

by floods that gather weight and speed,
revealing sky where massifs were,
in their desire to chisel free
through cuts and scars, towards the surf.

Water seeks the steepest fall,
but by its own descent, it slows,
held back in aquifers and lakes

and plains – its downward progress stalled
by its own freight of mud and stones.
Quietly, the sea evaporates.

FIRE

Quietly, the sea evaporates
at sun's command, rising as mist
which darkens, cools and gathers weight
to fall, then quails from earth's hot kiss

as lava overflows the torn
and scorched terrain - a dragon's tongue
that boils the surf as pumice forms,
in homage paid by earth to sun.

We bring to light the sun's lost hoard,
burn it, and pay our homage too,
exalting how the dragons' breath

we mimic, cools the dragon's core,
and warms the coldest place in view:
warmth kindled by the dragon's death.

AIR

Warmth kindled by the dragon's death
kisses your face – the rustling leaves
draw from it all they ask, and bless
the breeze with magic as they breathe.

It fills your new-born lungs in turn,
with grasping cries, and quiet sounds,
and tunes you half recall, and yearn
to sing and hear again, aloud.

The wind that blows across your smile
gives form to distant drifts and dunes,
floats words and seeds where they might grow

or parch or rot, and in those miles
becomes sirocco or monsoon,
shaping a world it doesn't know.

TISTA AUSTIN

FEN ORCHID

Nothing lights the way ahead
as the quest you've set yourself
to find the flower among the woods
of alder carr and reed beds at Sutton fen
before the summer ends

in places where you forget
until a yellow ghost like the paper
strewn across your desk drifts back
as a dream of something lost
reappears, slightly crumpled,

lips parted in a kiss,
grass-lit, under your touch
the slenderest taper of candle-shiver
which flowered on green-gold water
beside the blades of sedge-cutters.

SCHWANENGESANG

When all the votes have been lost and they're protesting
in Parliament Square, we take that road past the kennels,
so narrow it would be dangerous to drive in winter or the dark.

Is the water happy to flow here? you ask, of the streams
channelled into slow movements between the bulrushes
in a mash of spring buds and a shawl of mud.

No sound is coming from the water, no call
or roar of foam, as if a thought had fallen and sunk
like stone while louder traffic noises drowned its voice.

Nature seems untouched where mute swans are nesting
on scabious and wild ducks are wheeling over a ruined church
and the blurred glimpse of the village in the distance;

but there are no reflections in the waveless brook
dragging its way like a smoker's breath – only bottles
from energy drinks or discarded packets of medicine

going backwards and forwards like little boats,
pushing something silent and suffering into the riverbank.
History comes like a disruptive lover startling the landscape

where we walk alone on an unknown road, build a home
on the broken stair, search for eloquence in a word
choking the throat, tear off the roof and listen to the air.

BLUE FEN

There is nothing to see among the swards of water and ash
but this blue-dark crop, opaque colours like when you wake
or a mine of quartz, like a hurt hid deep.

I imagine workers on the splintered boardwalk planks
lined with creosote behind the irrigation machines,
maintaining the mosaic management, from realms
of water mint to these acres of cyan.
                                        I show you from the train,
a wattle fabric unstitched, a smoking bonfire unlit,
unpicked cobs and kernels of a blue corn
that will bring no warmth in winter, chaffing the skin
in the first white hoar and the blue fen wind.

Take these sheaves from my hands, cut without knives
to something unhealed; like a lover undressed from rough hessian threads,
leaves of diesel dark strands.

ANOTHER RIVER PATH

I went along another path because the bridge was closed
but still followed a wooded brook which seemed to course
towards a place where nature catches you with love
and almost doesn't hurt.
                         And all along
that gleaming bed which twists around
like long green hair while shadows split
like adders' tongues, I found you
in washed music sounds diving with the swallow.
Now in my room I write and trace
that restless stream to dig a track to your black room,
your blue chair with the torn brocade, the low roof
and all the wounds;
                             next time I'll bring you to the water's edge
bursting through clay-sodden steps with burnet rose
towards a world of amethyst which no one has yet found.

FERAL

We meant to cool off in the heatwave, wade
ankle deep in a stream, find a quiet spot
but forgot that the schools had just broken up:
kids on the bridge and the pier, shaved heads,
stripped bare –
     everywhere you looked
no place was clear, ten boys to a girl,
showing their bravery, launching their bikes
from the banks to the river, cartwheels
off pillars, cries catching damselflies,
paying scant heed to warnings
of danger, the currant lustrous,
quartz-bright;
     we thought our lives
were lived in this light where marsh roses grow
and there's nothing to fear.

       A surprise then
when one girl whirled round, spat out
we were perverts filming her tits,
(whilst her friend sneered she had none -),
demanded the camera, eyes sharper than briars;
her temper, trailed like a ghoul in the air, a rent
no will could repair.
     Days later
I passed a rivulet where a swan and four cygnets
streamed in a ditch bordered
by bog thistle, somehow burnished –
diving and diving and rising,
       the same pattern
shaken from circles of water, niches,
trying out wing skills, taking their chances,
until I was spied stood on the verge, unnatural
to that world;
     hissed at until I departed.